D0819502

*A visual collection
of the grandeur of the
Diablo-San Ramon Valley.*

Diablo Shadows

The sights, scenes and images
that encompass Alamo, Blackhawk, Danville, Diablo,
San Ramon & Walnut Creek.

SPONSORED BY
THE DANVILLE AREA CHAMBER OF COMMERCE
SAN RAMON CHAMBER OF COMMERCE, MT. DIABLO NATIONAL BANK
COLDWELL-BANKER & LAWRENCE VOLVO

Diablo Shadows

Contents

Diablo Shadows

Book designed and published by
Robert Pease & Company,
Post Office Box 1432
Alamo, California 94507

All rights reserved. No part of this publication may be reproduced or transmitted in any form or by any means, electronic or mechanical, including photocopy, recording or any information storage and retrieval system, without expressed permission of the publisher.

Library of Congress Cataloging in Publication Data.
Diablo Shadows
Library of Congress Catalog Card No. 98-92317
ISBN 0-9669310-0-9

Printed in the United States of America
© 1998 Robert Pease & Company

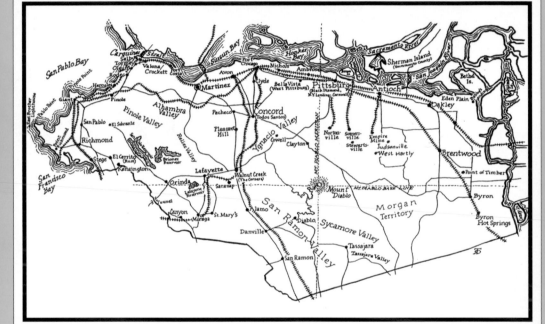

Diablo Shadows

by

ROBERT PEASE & WILLIAM HOCKINS

Foreward

SENATOR JOHN A. NEJEDLY

Introduction

HAL LARSON

Scenic Photography

WILLIAM HOCKINS

Graphic Design & Art Direction

ROBERT PEASE

Editor

MICHAEL SCOTT

Design & Production Associate

DAVID HARTZHEIM

Printer

GRAPHIC CENTER

Publisher

ROBERT PEASE & COMPANY

Quotations

FROM *LEAVES OF GRASS* BY WALT WHITMAN

DIABLO SHADOWS is not dry, historic record. It is not a vanity tome trumpeting local merchants and "first families." Rather, DIABLO SHADOWS is a stirring visual celebration of our own Mt. Diablo, its surrounding countryside and communities, among the most storied and desirable regions of our country. This loving, elegant tribute is the work of two nationally recognized artists: photographer Bill Hockins and graphic designer Robert Pease, both of whom have lived and worked at the foot of Mt. Diablo most of their lives.

Whether longtime resident or new arrival, we think you'll agree that, given this area's scenic and commercial bounty, there is much to

celebrate. As if the subtle yet ever-changing magnificence of the East Bay's towering peak is not reward enough, our towns host and share educational and cultural opportunities second to none.

We can boast highly acclaimed community colleges: Diablo Valley, Contra Costa, Los Medanos, Los Positas; four-year colleges and graduate schools including St. Mary's, JFK University, San Francisco State, University of Phoenix, Cal State Hayward, USF and UC Berkeley extensions, and the Regional Occupational Program (ROP).

We have world-class performing arts at the California Shakespeare Festival, California Symphony, Diablo Light Opera Company, and Walnut Creek's Dean Lesher Regional Center for the Arts.

We have shopping which some suggest renders San Francisco superfluous. But our greatest asset is the land itself, whether remaining tracts of open space or our protected East Bay Regional Park District, Las Trampas Regional Wilderness, and of course, Mt. Diablo State Park.

The quiet beauty of Mt. Diablo, the fertile Diablo Valley and environs attracted one of the East Bay's most illustrious residents, naturalist John Muir, whose books and magazine articles led to the creation of the National Park System and the Sierra Club, of which Muir was both cofounder and first president. John Muir was also friend and advisor to Theodore Roosevelt, who preserved more of America the Beautiful in national parks than any other president.

The view from Mt. Diablo in clearest weather extends 135 miles east/southeast to Yosemite National Park, west to the Farallon Islands 25 miles offshore, north 165 miles to Mt. Lassen, and south to Mt. Hamilton.

This panorama encompasses 20,000 to claims of 40,000 square miles, or more than the entire area of the state of Virginia. In 1851, Col. Leander Ransome, a US Army civil engineer, placed the original survey marker atop 3,849-foot Mt. Diablo for the base and meridian lines that measure most of California and all of Nevada. The US Government first surveyed California in 1876 using Mt. Diablo as base point.

As our population soars, we face the enormous challenge of balancing opportunity with respect for the land, water and air which nurture us all. The foundation for our quality of life; what supports our homes, schools, businesses, what sustains *us*, is and has always been, the *land*, from Mt. Diablo's oft snowcapped summit to the creeks rushing through unspoiled meadows of valley oak, wild lilac, mustard and rosemary. May this book open, and reopen, many eyes to our realm, and help further a reverence for the inherent beauty of Diablo country.

In 1865-66, the combined enrollment of all Danville-Alamo-San Ramon schools was 113 pupils. Today, it is over 20,000 students. They and the land are our real legacy. How we care for them both will be our lasting story.

SENATOR JOHN A. NEJEDLY
WALNUT CREEK, CALIFORNIA
November 1998

Circa 1890—
Elliot Publishing Co.,
San Francisco.

MOUNT DIABLO

THE peak was christened by the early Spaniards, and the name Diablo signifies that the genius of the mountain is no less than the devil, that being the meaning of the word.

Prof. Whitney, late Geologist of the State of California, said: "Mount Diablo presents itself in all its symmetry and grandeur, rising directly from the level of the sea. The view from the summit is magnificent—beyond description. Standing there on a clear day, and overlooking the craggy precipices and deep ravines, which impart an air of wild grandeur to the immediate vicinity, around the base of the mountain you behold, in all the elegance of their graceful outline and the beauty of their light and shadow, the admirably rounded foothills, gradually diminishing in prominence until they merge with the delightful valleys through whose groves of wide-spreading oaks and sycamores the eye involuntarily traces out the meandering courses of the sparkling waters, that after having dashed down their rugged mountain channels, appear to delight to linger amid the scenes of dreamy beauty with which they are surrounded."

Bill Hockins has been capturing the unique character of the Mount Diablo area on film since 1947.

Now, these priceless images have been compiled by Hockins and Art Director Robert Pease in this landmark work DIABLO SHADOWS. Pease says, "It is the definitive record of what has happened in the Valley this past half-century."

The handsome book includes scenes from Walnut Creek, Alamo, Diablo, Blackhawk, Danville and San Ramon. It records the ever-changing character of this lovely and historic area.

Certain to become a valued collector's item, the folio is the collaborative effort of two uncommonly gifted residents of the section chronicled in the book.

Hockins is a nationally known photographer and naturalist who fell in love with the changing patterns and colors of Diablo as a boy. He has been photographing it ever since. "The book," he says, "is an emotional trip back in time."

Bob Pease, like his collaborator, a resident of Alamo, is a celebrated Art Director and Publisher. His two girls grew up in the showcase home he built some 30 years ago. "DIABLO SHADOWS," he says, "is a true labor of love. I think everyone will be moved by Bill's remarkable photographs."

For both, the book is tinged with a sweet sadness, "It used to be rolling hills and farms and dazzling colors," says Hockins. "We've lost a lot of that incredible natural beauty."

Pease agrees but points out that it is not really lost. "It's all right here, between the covers of this book."

HAL LARSON
San Francisco

Too many people shared memories and information for us to ever thank individually, though we are grateful all the same and trust they will enjoy our effort.

Meanwhile, our special gratitude to Louise Bissett, James & Irma M. Dotson, Bill Fereira, Howard Fereira, Bob Fracolli, George Freese, Sheridan W. Hale, Virgie Jones, Le May (Al) Podva, Contra Costa Historical Society, Museum of the San Ramon Valley and Robin Welch of Airview Specialists, for historical detail and perspective; to Sandee Wiedemann La Violette for her *Recollections of San Ramon*; to Cindy and Jim Lawrence for period photographs and support.

Special thanks to: Linda Brewer, Nancy McCaffery, Jill Morrow, & Rick Peterson.

Last but not least, to David Hartzheim and Lorraine M. Pease for their steadfast dedication to the production of this folio.

For further reading, we heartily recommend *Danville: Portrait of 125 Years*, a publication of the Town of Danville, Robert Pease & Co. publisher, © 1984-85, Alamo...

Old Times in Contra Costa: A Journey to the Past, by Robert Daras Tatum, © 1993, Highland Publishers, Pittsburg, California...

Danville Branch of the Oakland Antioch & Eastern Railway, by Irma M. Dotson, © 1996, Museum of the San Ramon Valley, Danville, California.

1982—Snow on Mt. Diablo from El Pintado Road, Danville.

1987—Horse training track at Del Chase property above I-680 in Alamo.

1974—Woodbine subdivision from I-680 at Diablo Road.

1987—Oak tree in a field of mustard, La Gonda Way, Danville.

1976—Danville Boulevard, Danville.

12   *1980—Andy Anderson's ranch on Sycamore Road, Danville.*

1989—Bailed hay, Highland Road, Danville.

1979—Barn, Tassajara Road, Danville.

1997—San Ramon development.

"Long and long has the grass been growing,
Long and long has the rain been falling,
Long has the globe been rolling round."

13

1976—Side hay rake,
Wiedermann Ranch, San Ramon
(now Bishop Ranch Business Park).

"To behold the daybreak!
The little light fades the immense and diaphanous shadows,
The air tastes good to my palate."

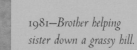

1981—Brother helping
sister down a grassy hill.

End of Green Valley Road,
Bryan Ranch area, as seen
from Round Hill north, Alamo.

1955—Danville Feed & Supply.
Former railroad depot,
currently being restored as
San Ramon Valley Museum.

Marissa Gomez
waiting for a school bus,
Finley Road, Alamo.

1988—The end of the July 4th parade, Danville. Shooting it up by The Devil Mountain Brigade.

1978—Check dam at Front Street and East Prospect, Danville.

1976—Mt. Diablo from
Castle Crest Road, Alamo.

ALAMO

IF tranquil Alamo seems lost between its more populous, bustling neighbors, adjoining Danville and Walnut Creek, that's just fine with most Alamoans. Alamo natives take pride that their little unincorporated township hosted the San Ramon Valley's first post office back in 1852. The post office, the only one between Martinez and Mission San Jose, was in postmaster John M. Jones' adobe home, across the road from today's Alamo Plaza. Alamo still enjoys an off the beaten path atmosphere, the old two-lane "Danville Highway" (Hwy 21) remaining the principal thoroughfare.

Among the smaller towns in Diablo's shadow (population 12,277), Alamo straddles former orchards and wheat fields now arrayed with quiet neighborhoods of ranch homes. One of these secluded lanes, Castle Crest Road, is the steepest paved street in Contra Costa County. Castle Crest climbs a third of Mt. Diablo's west face, rivaling San Francisco's infamous Filbert Street, whose steepest incline was for years the ruling grade for Detroit's automakers. As Alamo's shrubbed slopes and valleys enter the 21st century, they are home not only to successful managers, educators and high-tech professionals, but to small working family farms and equestrians.

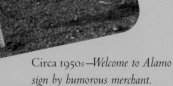

Circa 1950s—Welcome to Alamo
sign by humorous merchant.

1974–I-680 at Stone Valley Road, Alamo.

Circa 1900–Alamo Post Office on Danville Highway.

1939–Davies photo of homes in Alamo.

Circa 1900–Joe Lawrence in front of Henry Hotel, Alamo.

Circa 1900—*Arbor of grapevines, Alamo.*

1976—*Flying "A" gas station and Alamo Gardens Motel, Danville Blvd., Alamo.*

1989—*Very old house on Livorna Road, Alamo.*

1975—"S" curve on
Stone Valley Road
and Alta Sierra
Place, Alamo.

1974—Local fawna
grazing above
Round Hill,
Alamo.

1974—LPGA National
Women's Golf Tourney,
Round Hill Country
Club, Alamo.

1979—
Fog creeping into
the valley, Alamo.

1989—*Waterfall, Del Chase ranch, Alamo.*

"O love and summer! you are in the dreams and in me,
Autumn and winter are in the dreams....
the farmer goes with his thrift,
The droves and crops increase....
the barns are wellfilled."

1985—*The last barn,
Round Hill North,
Alamo.*

21

1975—Alamo Feed and antique store, downtown Alamo.

1986—Sunburst grass painting above Stone Valley Road, Alamo.

1976—Stone Valley Center, Alamo, with snow on Mt. Diablo.

1976—I-680 off-ramp at Stone Valley Road, Alamo.

1975—I-680 Freeway, Alamo.

Circa 1920—(left to right)
Campbell House, Alamo.
Originally a bunkhouse for
Rancho San Ramon prior to
1849 California statehood.
In the late 1800s, it became
a walnut farm. Today, the
original barn and carriage
house still exist.

1998—Round Hill North, Alamo.

1987—Tunnel to
Del Chase Ranch, Alamo.

1973—Round Hill Country Club, Alamo.

1990—Henry Building, Alamo Coffee Shop, Danville Blvd., Alamo.

1973—Entrance to Round Hill Country Club, Alamo.

1971—14th Fairway, Round Hill Country Club, Alamo.

1985—*Feeder barn of the John Bryan Ranch, Alamo.*

1983—*Alamo Plaza Shopping Center, Alamo.*

1977—*Round Hill Country Club, Alamo.*

1976—*Snow on Mt. Diablo.*

1961—I-680 Freeway
ended at Rudgear
Road, Alamo.

1975—Round Hill Country
Club entrance on Stone Valley
Road, Alamo.

1975—Stone Valley Center
and I-680, Alamo.

1975—Wes Bailey
home above Stone
Valley Road, Alamo.

"Dazzling and tremendous how quick
the sunrise would kill me,
If I could not now and always send
sunrise out of me.

We also ascend dazzling
and tremendous as the sun,
We found our own my soul
in the calm and cool of the daybreak."

1977—Overlooking Stone Valley Road, Alamo.

1974—Construction of 17th Fairway, Round Hill Country Club, Alamo.

1974—I-680 and Alamo Plaza Center, Alamo.

1973—Oak tree, Castle Crest Road, Alamo.

"O the gleesome saunter over fields and hillsides!
The leaves and flowers of the commonest weeds,
the moist fresh stillness of the woods,
The exquisite smell of the earth at daybreak,
and all through the forenoon."

*1974—Mt. Diablo
with hikers.*

*1976—Rustic barn
in the hills of Alamo.*

*1963—13th Green,
Round Hill Country Club,
Alamo.*

*1976—Horse in
a hay field, Alamo.*

29

1998—
Round Hill North,
Alamo.

1974—
Stone Valley Road,
Alamo.

1974—
Clouds on
Mt. Diablo.

1939—
Davies photo,
Henry Hotel,
Alamo.

1967—Overlooking the
top of Castle Crest Road
"The Hill" development, Alamo.

1997—San Ramon Valley
Iron Horse Regional Trail,
bike and jogging path,
Alamo.

1967—First home under
construction on "The Hill,"
Castle Crest Road, Alamo.

1984—Sunset behind Oak Tree in Walnut Creek

1998—Diablo Country Club, 4th green, Diablo.

1998—Blackhawk Automotive Museum, Blackhawk Plaza.

(Opposite) Sunshine on green hills, Tassajara Road, Danville.   *(Above) 1985—Mt. Diablo from Round Hill, Alamo.*

1976—*Salt block rack*
for Hap Magee cattle on
Hidden Oak area, Danville.

34

Horse barn on Hansen Lane, now Blackhawk.

1978—Mt. Diablo Greenbrook area, Danville.

1980—Old wagon on Podva Ranch, Danville.

"A child said, What is the grass? fetching to me with full hands;
How could I answer the child? I do not know what it is any more than he.
I guess it must be the flag of my disposition, out of hopeful green stuff wove
Or I guess the grass it itself a child, the produced babe of the vegetation."

*Mustard, almond trees
and Las Trampas hills.*

1978—*Feeder barn on
Green Valley Road, Danville.*

"The flashing and golden pageant of California,
The sudden and gorgeous drama,
the sunny and ample lands,
Lands bathed in sweeter, rarer,
healthier air, valleys and mountain cliffs,
The fields of Nature long prepared and fallow,
the silent, cyclic chemistry,
The slow and steady ages plodding,
the unoccupied surface ripening,
the rich ores forming beneath;
At last the New arriving, taking possession."

1982—*Snow
on Mt. Diablo
from Woodbine
subdivision, Danville.*

1987—Pacific Bell complex at San Ramon's Bishop Ranch.

Wisp of fog on Mt. Diablo foothills.

37

1988—July 4th parade, Danville.

1980—Mustard and eucalyptus frame Mt. Diablo from Bethel Island.

1997—
Bishop Ranch
office complex and
Las Trampas hills,
SanRamon.

1998—
San Ramon Park.

*1976—Hay barn on
Wiedermann Ranch,
San Ramon (now Bishop
Ranch office complex).*

*1998—Footbridge from
Danville Boulevard to
Hap Magee Park, Danville.*

*Devil Mountain Run,
Greenbrook, Danville.*

"I hear the workman singing and the farmer's wife singing
I hear in the distance the sounds of children and of animals early in the day."

BLACKHAWK

IN 1916, Ansel Mills Easton, a Hillsborough millionaire, founded the Blackhawk Ranch on 1,250 acres bought from Robert N. Burgess, owner of Oakwood Park Stock Farm (see Diablo). For 18 years, Easton raised shire draft horses and shorthorn cattle here.

The retired president of Caterpillar Tractor, Raymond C. Force, bought Blackhawk in 1934, adding Arabian horses and Hereford cattle.

In 1956, Blackhawk passed to pineapple growers Castle & Cook Ltd. and Helemano Co., Ltd., Honolulu.

In 1964, G. Howard Peterson, of Peterson Tractor, the northern California Caterpillar dealers, bought Blackhawk, in turn selling most of it, in 1972, to a Florida mobile home entrepreneur and real estate developer, Ken Behring, who developed the property into custom homes, offices and shopping centers.

Blackhawk Plaza is the site of interesting shops and elegant restaurants, adjacent to the internationally renowned Blackhawk Automotive Museum. The museum, which is affiliated with the University of California at Berkeley, covers a century of rare, restored automobiles and motoring artifacts.

1990—Windmill and barn on Camino Tassajara and Lawrence Road, now Blackhawk.

1974- View of Blackhawk from Bee Man Ridge, Danville.

41

1987—Rancher Al (Le May) Podva at Hansen Barn, Blackhawk area, Danville.

1995—Bugatti racer, Blackhawk Automotive Museum, Danville.

1998—Blackhawk Automotive Museum, Danville.

1986—Blackhawk development with Falls Golf Course, far right.

1993—Homes under construction in Blackhawk, Danville.

1998—Blackhawk Grille, Danville.

Circa 1980s— 18th Green, Lake Course, Blackhawk Golf Course, Danville.

1976— Horses on Mt. Diablo foothills.

1984— Clubhouse at Lake Course, Blackhawk Country Club, Danville.

1984—*Entrance to Blackhawk, Danville.*

1982—*Mt. Diablo grass fire behind Blackhawk, Danville.*

1998—*Blackhawk Automotive Museum, Danville.*

1998—*Rare cars on exhibit, Blackhawk Automotive Museum, Danville.*

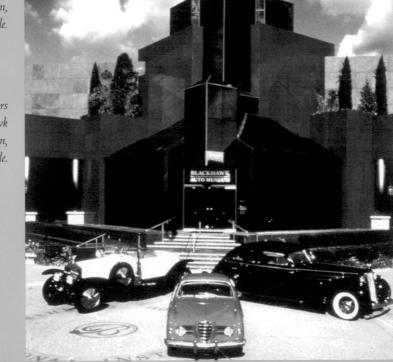

"The press of my foot to the earth
springs a hundred affections,
They scorn the best
I can do to relate them."

1974—
Last shipment
of cattle from
Blackhawk Ranch,
Danville.

45

1998—Part of the fabulous
car collection on display,
Blackhawk Automotive Museum,
Danville.

1976—
Last harvesting of barley
at Blackhawk Ranch, near
what is now the main entrance to
Blackhawk Country Club, Danville.

DANVILLE

DPERHAPS no community better blends abiding respect for a disappearing rural past with controlled growth and colorful, family-owned businesses, than the Town of Danville, population 38,104. At once quaint and vibrant, Danville's downtown is a sterling example of farsighted city planning. Wishing to preserve a small-town aesthetic in the face of encroaching overdevelopment, in 1982 the Town of Danville incorporated.

The new town council wisely protects historic Danville while working with businesses able to appreciate the big picture. This smart, respectful approach is placed in historic perspective if we remember that many of the town's original settlers were miners recovering from "gold fever," and were now willing to cast their lot with the rolling farmland. So don't be surprised to see schools, progressive companies, and comfortable homes alongside working cattle ranches, orchards, and truck farms.

America's greatest playwright, Eugene O'Neill, used part of his 1936 Nobel Prize money to build a home at the upper end of Kuss Road. There, from his study with its inspiring view of Mt. Diablo, O'Neill wrote *The Iceman Cometh, Long Day's Journey into Night, Hughie,* and his last play, *Moon for the Misbegotten,* winner of four Tony Awards in 1974. Tours of the Eugene O'Neill National Historic Site may be arranged by calling (925) 838-0249.

Circa 1890s–Shuey's Warehouse and Ranch, Danville.

1956–Snow on Mt. Diablo from Woodbine Subdivision, Danville.

"Come now I will not be tantalized....
you conceive too much of articulation."

1976—Mt. Diablo with
a dusting of snow from
Diablo Road, Danville.

Circa 1980s—
Welcome to Danville sign.

WELCOME TO
DANVILLE

ROTARY CLUB
LIONS CLUB
SOROPTIMISTS
KIWANIS CLUB

1940—Downtown
Danville.

48

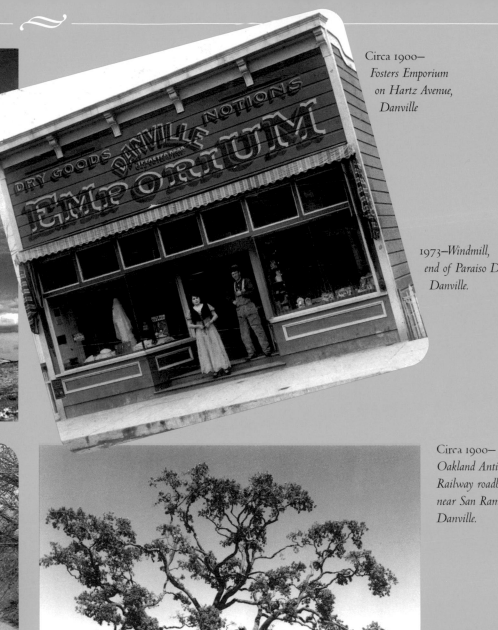

Circa 1900—
*Fosters Emporium
on Hartz Avenue,
Danville*

1973—*Windmill,
end of Paraiso Drive,
Danville.*

Circa 1900—
*Oakland Antioch & Eastern
Railway roadbed washed out
near San Ramon High School,
Danville.*

1980—
*Danville Christmas oak
on Diablo Road.*

HARTZ AVENUE DANVILLE CAL.

Circa 1900—
Hartz Avenue,
looking south from
Prospect Street,
Danville.

Circa 1900—
Toll gate at
Mt. Diablo State Park,
Danville.

1956—Snow on
Mt. Diablo from
Danville.

"Encompass worlds
but never try to encompass me,
I crowd your noisiest talk
by looking toward you."

1958—July 4th parade,
prototype jet engines
from GE, Danville.

1976—
Snow in Danville.

1977—
Podva Home, now
Danville Livery & Merchantile.

51

Circa 1900—
*Dubbed the
Toonerville Trolley,
on Hartz Avenue,
Oakland Antioch & Eastern
Railway, Danville.*

1975—
*Danville Feed (Ramos),
Danville.*

Circa 1900—
*Hiram Elliott's Home,
Diablo Street, renamed
Diablo Road,
Danville.*

1940—
*American Legion Follies,
Danville.*

DANVILLE MACHINE WORKS
ELECTRICAL SUPPLIES and HOUSE WIRING
AGENTS FOR GAS ENGINES and MOTORS
WIND MILLS and PUMPS
WELL BORING PLUMBING Etc.   GARAGE

Circa 1900—
Danville Machine Shop,
Danville.

1974—Looking
down on Danville
from Bee Man Ridge,
Blackhawk.

1955–"Hay Days Parade,"
later became July 4th event, Danville.

Circa 1900–St. Isidore Church,
Hartz Avenue & Linda Mesa, Danville.

Circa 1900–San Ramon Valley Bank, Hartz & E. Prospect,
(now a Starbucks coffee shop), Danville.

"The earth by the sky staid with....the daily close of their junction,
The heaved challenge from the east that moment over my head,
The mocking taunt, See then whether you shall be master!"

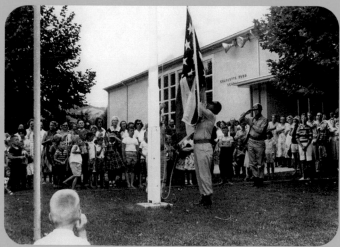

Circa 1912—
Alamo Grammar School.

1940—Hartz Avenue,
looking south, Danville

1960—July 4th, flag raising,
Charlotte Wood School, Danville.

*1982—Tassajara School,
built in 1865, Danville.*

*1976—A.J. Young home.
Now remodeled at the
Danville-San Ramon
Medical Center,
Danville.*

*1958—100th.
anniversary of Danville,
Miss Pioneer Belle Contest.*

1975—Mt. Diablo from
Castanya Court, Danville.

1976—Windmill and tank,
Lawrence Road, Blackhawk,
Danville.

57

1974–169 *Front Street,
Insurance by Hockins Building,
Danville.*

1981–*Mt. Diablo
foothills with house
under construction.*

1979–
*Culvert near
Educational Center,
Danville.*

"I hear the bravuras of birds....the bustle of growing wheat....
gossip of flames....clack of sticks cooking my meals.

I hear the sound of the human voice....a sound I love,
I hear all sounds as they are tuned to their uses....sounds of the
city and sounds out of the city....sounds of the day and night."

Mid 1970s—
*Last cutting of barley
at Blackhawk Ranch,
Danville.*

Circa 1890—*Livery stable,
built by John Halverson,
Danville.*

Circa 1900—*Smith Ranch,
Alamo Oaks,
Danville.*

1974—
*Ellsworthy Ranch,
Danville.*

"O love and summer! you are in the dreams and in me,
Autumn and winter are in the dreams....the farmer goes with his thrift,
The droves and crops increase...the barns are wellfilled."

Mid 1950s—*Parade rider gets a close shave enroute! Danville.*

1976—*Sycamore Road overcrossing, looking west to Las Trampas Range, Danville.*

1948—*Harlan Geldermann and friends waiting for the July 4th parade, Danville.*

1975—Danville Hotel, Danville.

Circa 1970s—
Rear of Danville Hotel, Danville.

1958—Danville resident, Joe Silva, drives Miss Pioneer Belle, Ingrid Schadt, and her court in Danville 100th anniversary parade.

1977—Danville Hotel Territory Shops, Danville.

Circa 1970s—
*Danville Hotel,
Danville.*

DANVILLE HOTEL . GEO. E. McCAULEY. PROP.

Circa 1890—
*Early engraving of
Danville Hotel.*

1997—
*Hartz Avenue.,
downtown Danville.*

1998—
*Hot August Nights,
Danville.*

1998—
*City Hall & Administration,
Danville.*

1976—
*Podva Barn,
Danville.*

1987—Barn and horse,
Hansen Lane,
Blackhawk area,
Danville.

1996—Bear carving from
tree stump, Danville.

Circa 1900—
Olson Garage,
Hartz and
Diablo Road,
Danville.

65

1977—Podva barn, now site of
Danville Livery & Mercantile,
Danville.

Circa 1990—
Danville Post Office
on Tassajara Road.

Circa 1960s—
*July 4th parade,
Danville.*

1975—
*Tassajara School
on Finley Road,
Danville.*

Circa 1930s—
*Mt. Diablo toll gate,
Danville.*

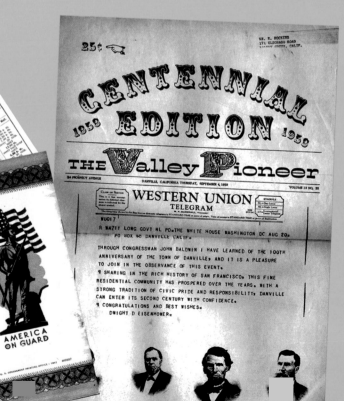

Circa 1916—
Electric rail line near entrance into
Diablo Club Properties; racetrack
in background, Diablo.

Circa 1920—Railway workers
on track to Diablo, presently near St.
Timothy's Episcopal Church,
Danville.

1975—I-680 ends
at Rudgear Road,
Alamo.

DIABLO

HARNESS racing was serious sport in San Ramon Valley at the opening of the 20th century. Some of the world's fastest trotters were bred at the 6,000-acre Oakwood Park Stock Farm, which included all of what became Diablo, as well as the southern slopes of Mt. Diablo nearly to the summit. As the automobile age, and more residents arrived, the stock farm was converted to a country club after 1912, seat of the rustic community of Diablo.

In the 1920s and '30s, many San Franciscans summered at their Diablo "country" homes. Many of these survive, though oft remodeled and with added rooms and wings. The impressive Diablo Country Club, beautifully restored and maintained, continues serving diners, dancers, golfers and tennis players the genteel good life much as it did nearly 90 years ago.

Diablo's tree-lined, speed-bumped streets wind past homes new and old in a stunning variety of architectural styles. This is one suburban town where it is still possible, on any afternoon, to hear no sounds beyond a barking dog, crickets, birds, the occasional clip-clop of horse hooves, punctuated only by the periodic passing of a resident's car.

From 1914 to '24, an electric trolley named for a popular comic strip, The Toonerville Trolley, ran between Walnut Creek and Diablo, until it, too, lost out to the automobile.

1955–
*Diablo Country Club,
Diablo.*

Circa 1900—
Red horse barn,
Diablo.

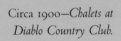

Circa 1900—*Chalets at*
Diablo Country Club.

Circa 1900—
Harvesting sugar beets,
Baldwin Ranch,
Danville.

1993—
Hap Magee cattle
at rest, Diablo.

1974—
Hap Magee cattle,
Diablo.

1955—
Mt. Diablo
from the air.

Circa 1920s—
Diablo Country Club,
Diablo.

1916—
Oakland Antioch & Eastern
Railway electric train stopped
in Diablo.

1976—
*Looking back at 1st Tee,
Diablo Country Club.*

Circa 1916—*tickets and
billboard for Danville branch of
Oakland Antioch & Eastern Railway
"One Day Trip to Mt. Diablo" from
San Francisco.*

1950—
*"Flat Top" Smith Compound,
Diablo Country Club.*

"Peace is always beautiful,
The myth of heaven indicates peace and night."

*Las Trampas hills,
almond orchard and
field of mustard,
Danville.*

1985—
*Western artifacts on
barn side, Danville.*

1977—
*McPhearson barn on
Highland Drive.*

1981—
*Mt. Diablo from
Round Hill north,
Alamo.*

1982—
*Snow on Mt. Diablo from
Antioch Golf Course.*

(Top) 1987—Clouds over Danville.

(Bottom left) 1992—Residents feeding
ducks at Oak Hill Park, Danville.

(Bottom right) 1985—Rusty barn
door hinge, Hanson Lane, Blackhawk.

*1986—Sunrise at
Oak Hill Park,
Stone Valley Road,
Danville.*

"If you bring the warmth of the sun to them
they will open and bring form, color, perfume, to you,
If you become the aliment and the wet
they will become flowers, fruits, tall branches, and trees."

1992—Snow on Mt. Diablo foothills.

1987—Del Chase Ranch
at the end of La Gonda
Way, Danville.

1987—Pacific Bell
complex in Bishop Ranch,
San Ramon.

1980—Sunset behind
Mormon Church on
Stone Valley Road, Alamo.

Mt. Diablo from Dougherty Road
area, San Ramon.

1989—
Snow on Mt. Diablo
from San Ramon.

1974—
Tank house on
Castle Crest Road,
Walnut Creek.

Oak Hill Park
on Stone Valley
Road, Danville.

1975—
Last cutting of barley
on Blackhawk Ranch.

1998—
Blackhawk Grill at
Blackhawk Plaza.

1997—
BART train,
Walnut Creek Sation.

1995—
Devil Mountain
Run, Greenbrook
area, Danville.

1981—Mt. Diablo
from Orinda.

1993—
Water tank on Morgan Territory Road.

1998—
Dean Lesher Regional Center for the Arts, Walnut Creek.

1988—
July 4th parade, Danville.

SAN RAMON

NAMED Brevensville for its first blacksmith, then Lynchville after an early settler, and for decades Limerick for the growing Irish population, "San Ramon" was always the titular contender, dating from the 1830s, at least. The creek running from Bollinger Canyon shared the name with three Valley ranchos: Rancho San Ramon (Amador), Rancho San Ramon (Castro/Pacheco), and El Sobrante de San Ramon (Romero). Maria Amador, whose ranch included most of today's San Ramon, told in his memoirs how one of the oldest city names in California evolved. "The creek was so christened by a *mayordomo* named Ramon (of Mission San Jose in Fremont, one of the 21 Spanish missions established from 1769–1823)." Ramon had the care of some sheep where today graze office parks, Dodge Rams and Lexi.

Bishop Ranch hails from T. B. Bishop, a leading San Francisco corporate attorney of the 1880s and '90s, who bought 3,000 acres of what had been Rancho San Ramon. Bishop died in 1906, but his four sons began one of Contra Costa County's leading walnut groves, and in 1911 planted a pear orchard which became the largest single block of Bartlett pears in the world.

San Ramon's charms, hills and valleys blanketed with waist-high wild oats, clover, prodigious stands of oaks and maples, clean-running streams lined with willows and mottled-trunked sycamores, and a glory of bloom-eschscholtzia (California poppies), lupine and myriad other flowers, lured pre-Gold Rush home seekers to park their canvas-covered, ox-drawn wagons and pitch their tents at the base of Mt. Diablo. Today, the tents are sprawling, air-conditioned ranch homes, and to their owners' chagrin, new settlers keep pouring in.

The San Ramon sign said "Population 100" until 1965, when the Interstate (680) came. Well into the 1950s, children would get out of school in late September and October to help pick walnuts. One resident remembers attending second grade in San Ramon in 1953. Her brother was in first grade, their sister in third. All three were in the same room, taught by the same teacher, the principal. In 1959, there were a total six students in her eighth grade class, two girls, four boys.

From 1891–1907, as terminus for the Southern Pacific's Oakland Antioch Eastern line, San Ramon was the Valley's most prosperous community. Incorporated in 1983, San Ramon with a population today of 42,000 and climbing, is today trying to preserve some of its history, and to counter an image as the East Bay's service station, in late 1998 denying a permit to a chain of "lube & lattes."

Circa 1900s—
Thorup home in San Ramon.

Circa 1940s—
Hay bailing and threshers working on Henry Smith Ranch, San Ramon.

Circa 1890s—
H.C. Hurst General Merchandise, San Ramon.

Circa 1900s—
Henry Hurst General Store,
San Ramon.

1982—Bishop Ranch
from Greenbrook,
San Ramon.

GENERAL MERCHANDISE.

SAN RAMON POST OFFICE.

SAN RAMON
POP. 100 · · ELEV. 490

Circa 1940s—
San Ramon.

"I swear they are all beautiful,
Every one that sleeps is beautiful....every thing in the dim night
is beautiful,
The wildest and bloodiest is over and all is peace."

1993—*View from top of
85' aerial fire truck,
San Ramon.*

1976—*Construction starting on
Crow Canyon Country Club,
San Ramon.*

Circa 1920s—
*Bull rider in
San Ramon.*

Circa 1900s—
Methodist Church,
San Ramon.

Circa 1940s—
Hay bailing and threshers
working on Henry Smith Ranch,
San Ramon.

Circa 1900—
Geldermann home "El Nido,"
San Ramon.

"I am he that walks the tender and growing night;
I call to the earth and sea half-held by the night."

84

Circa 1920—
Fry Blacksmith Shop,
San Ramon.

1914—
San Ramon Valley High School,
Danville.

1974—
San Ramon Train Station,
San Ramon.

CASH - JOURNAL

THOMAS B. BISHOP CO.

85

Circa 1900s—Ed Majors with one of
the first automobiles in the valley.

1920—Metalsmith shop with metal silo,
Front Street, Danville.

(Opposite) 1982, Eastern side of Mt. Diablo.   (Above) Circa 1940—San Ramon Grammar School, San Ramon.

(Top) 1926—Bettencourt Ranch,
Blackhawk area, Danville.

(Bottom left) 1986—Barn and horse,
Morgan Territory Road.

(Bottom right) 1996—
San Ramon Community Park,
San Ramon.

1976—Cattle on Wiedemann Ranch,
now Canyon Lakes Country Club,
San Ramon

1992—Green hills of Alamo.

"The wild gander leads his flock through the cool night,
Ya-honk! he says, and sounds it down to me like an invitation;
The pert may suppose it meaningless, but I listen closer,
I find its purpose and place up there toward the November sky."

Circa 1900—
San Ramon Train Station,
San Ramon.

1927—
Group of San Ramon residents
standing next to San Ramon Jail.

Circa 1900—
Bishop Ranch,
walnut harvesting,
San Ramon.

Circa 1900—
Bishop Ranch crew,
San Ramon.

1912—
San Ramon Valley High School,
Danville.

Circa 1900—
Bishop Ranch,
walnut harvesting,
San Ramon.

"I think I will do nothing for a long time but listen,
And accrue what I hear into myself....and let sounds
contribute toward me."

Circa 1955—Looking west at
Crow Canyon Road and Alcosta Blvd.,
San Ramon.

1927—Cliff and Bill Fereira
in front of general store,
San Ramon.

1920—Prunes
drying in the sun,
San Ramon.

Circa 1900s—
Thorup Shoe Shop,
San Ramon.

1997—
San Ramon Community Park,
San Ramon.

Circa 1900s—*A.J. Young House,*
San Ramon Valley Blvd. and Podva Road,
Danville.

"What is commonest and cheapest and nearest and easiest is Me,
Me going in for my chances, spending for vast returns,
Adorning myself to bestow myself on the first that will take me,
Scattering it freely forever."

1978—*Present site of Creekside Community Church, Alamo.*

Circa 1900—
Geldermann home, "El Nido," San Ramon.

Circa 1900s—
Bishop Ranch cook house, San Ramon.

"Do you know how the buds beneath are folded?
Waiting in gloom protected by frost,
The dirt receding before my prophetical screams,
I underlying causes to balance them at last,
My knowledge my live parts....it keeping tally with the meaning of things,
Happiness....which whoever hears me let him or her set out in search of this day."

Circa 1900—
San Ramon Post Office, San Ramon.

94

1928—
William Fereira
with sons
Cliff and Bill
on first school bus
in San Ramon.

Circa 1900—
Ramona Park,
San Ramon.

1940—
San Ramon Hall,
San Ramon.

Danville, California

Circa 1950s—Downtown Danville.

98

1986—Summer from San Damiano, Danville.

1985—Christmas tree, Diablo Road, Danville.

1993—Mt. Diablo, Danville.

1996—Looking west at Las Trampas ridge, Rossmoor, from Castle Crest Road, Alamo

78—Spring from San Damiano overlooking, Danville.

1991—Poppies on Mt. Diablo off a fire trail, south side of the mountain.

1974—Fall on Mt. Diablo from Woodbine, Danville.

"O truth of the earth! O truth of things!
I am determined to press the whole way toward you,
Sound your voice! I scale mountains or dive in the sea after you."

99

1976—Mt. Diablo
from Education Center,
Danville.

1981—Mt. Diablo
from Mt. Diablo
Hospital roof.

1978—Hap Magee
long horn cattle,
Diablo.

1986—Mona Lisa
grass painting, Alamo.

"I am enamoured of growing outdoors,
Of men that live among cattle
or taste of the oceans or woods,
Of the builders and steerers of ships,
of the wielders of axes and mauls,
of the drivers of horses,
I can eat and sleep with them week in and week out.

1985—San Ramon.

1986—
Restored
Podva home,
Danville.

1992—BART train, Walnut Creek.

1982—Early development
of Bishop Ranch as seen
from Greenbrook, Danville.

1987—Lichen-covered
barn wall, Hansen Lane,
Blackhawk.

1997—13th tee, Round Hill
Country Club, Alamo.

1993—Tassajara School,
Finley Road, Danville.

1982—Snow on Mt. Diablo
from Round Hill north,
on Chanticleer Lane, Alamo.

WALNUT CREEK

WALNUT Creek's status as the Valley's mercantile hub is nothing new. First called The Corners, it was the spot where four Mexican land grants met, as well as the main crossroads of Contra Costa, where the Martinez-San Jose trail met the road from Oakland. These rutted roads, today known as Main Street and Mount Diablo Boulevard, became the county's first highways, later replaced by freeways 24 and 680. Named for the native black walnut trees lining the creeks, Walnut Creek became a town by 1860, incorporating in 1914.

Wheat farms became less profitable in the 1890s, grape production dropped with Prohibition, so miles of walnut groves sprung up in the 1920s. Walnut Creek's annual celebration was known as the Grape Festival until the '20s, and one of the town's biggest businesses into the '50s was a huge tomato canning plant at the site of today's Target department store. In 1920, the first year of Prohibition, local farmers organized the Contra Costa County Walnut Growers Association, building a processing and packing plant in Walnut Creek.

Additional plants opened in 1937 and '51. By 1958, there were 900 grower-members in Contra Costa, Alameda, Merced, and Stanislaus counties, when the now state association (since 1946 called Diamond Walnut Growers) moved operations to Stockton. Walnut Creek's plant remained for grading, sizing and bleaching.

The walnut groves have become bedrooms for lawyers, stockbrokers, bankers and corporate middle management, the original growers' warehouse now the site of the Lesher Regional Center for the Arts.

The Southern Pacific's San Ramon Valley branch line carried Walnut Creek passengers through 1912, and through the 1960s mail, freight, and produce from area farms, vineyards and orchards from Richmond, Martinez, Avon, Concord, Walnut Creek, Alamo, Danville, San Ramon, Livermore, Pleasanton, down Niles Canyon and back to Oakland and throughout the nation and the world. The Southern Pacific's still serviceable Walnut Creek tracks were dismantled in 1980 to make way for a jogging path. The Southern Pacific's Walnut Creek station survives as a steak house, amidst a profusion of downtown parking garages, trendy restaurants, and upmarket retailers like Macy's and Nordstrom.

Until 1941, commuters, shoppers, and visitors were whisked throughout Walnut Creek and Diablo country by smooth, quiet interurbans on the Oakland Antioch & Eastern (later Sacramento Northern) electric railway. The big, elegant, comfortable cars hummed not just to Isleton, Walnut Creek, Bay Point (Port Chicago), Pittsburg and San Ramon, but to Oakland, San Francisco, and at speeds up to 70 and 80 miles an hour, to Woodland, Marysville, Colusa and Chico.

1998— Highway 24 at Pleasant Hill Road, 5 p.m. traffic, Walnut Creek.

Circa 1920s— South Main Street, Walnut Creek.

Circa 1890s—
W. S. Burpee home,
Walnut Creek.

"The shapes arise!
The shape of the planks of the family room,
the home of the friendly parents and children,
The shape of the roof
of the happy young man and woman,
the roof over the well-married young man and woman,
The roof over the supper cook'd by the chaste wife,
and joyously eaten by the chaste husband,
content after his day's work."

Circa 1960—
Mt. Diablo and I-680
and Highway 24.

1955—
*Looking north over South Main
and Newell Ave.,
Walnut Creek.*

Circa 1920s—
*South Main Street,
Walnut Creek.*

Circa 1890—
*Rogers Hotel,
Walnut Creek.*

Circa 1890—
*Home and blacksmith shop
of M. Kirsch,
Walnut Creek.*

1956—
*Close-up view of
downtown Walnut Creek.*